GETTING TO KNOW JESUS

PATRICIA BRENNAN-NICHOLS

Argus Communications   A Division of DLM, Inc. Allen, Texas 75002 U.S.A.

Designed and illustrated by LYDIA HALVERSON

Copyright © 1984 Argus Communications

All rights reserved. No portion of this book may be reproduced, stored in a retrieval system, or transmitted in any form by any means—electronic, mechanical, photocopying, recording, or otherwise—without prior written permission of the copyright owner.

Printed in the United States of America

Argus Communications
A Division of DLM, Inc.
One DLM Park
Allen, Texas 75002 U.S.A.

International Standard Book Number: 0-89505-130-3

0 9 8 7 6 5 4 3 2 1

CONTENTS

1	Mary Says Yes	1
2	Shepherds Visit a King	7
3	The Star That Led to a King	15
4	Jesus Learns about Love	21
5	Jesus in His Father's House	27
6	Those Who Follow Jesus	35
7	Jesus Teaches about God's Love	43
8	Jesus' Healing Love	51
9	Jesus' Story about a Good Neighbor	57
10	Jesus Loves the Little Children	63

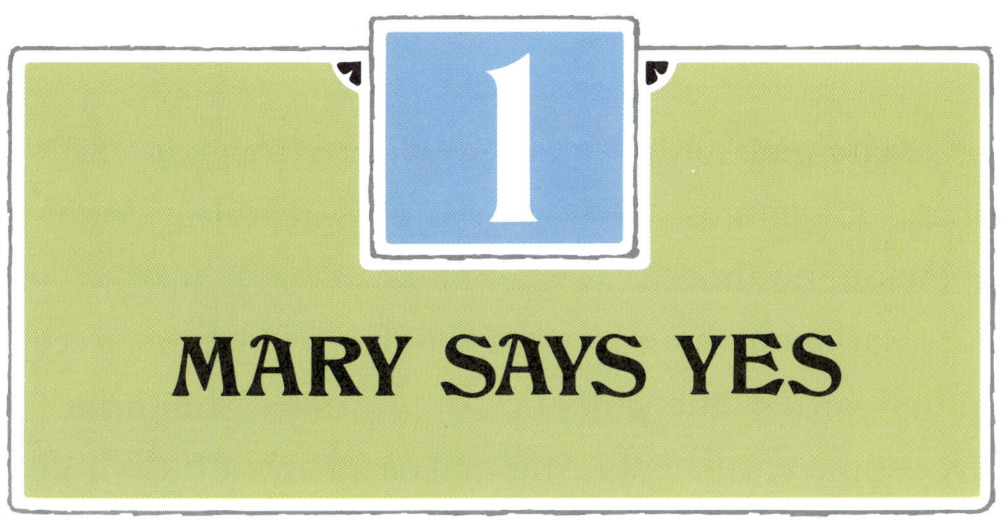

1
MARY SAYS YES

None of us was in Mary's garden when God's angel, Gabriel, came to visit her. He came to tell her about Jesus. The Bible tells us the important things that happened that day. But it's up to us to imagine what the day was like.

Imagine a small yard and garden next to a small house. The air is hot and dry. A young girl comes out of the house. It is Mary. She is looking for something. Oh! Mary is wearing only one sandal. Where is her other sandal?

Oh, no! The goat, Zev, is chewing on it. Mary sees him now. "Oh, dear," she says.

Mary grabs her sandal away from the goat. "Silly goat," she laughs. "If you are hungry, eat! But don't chew on my shoe!"

Mary pats the goat on the head. She begins to dig in her garden. She pulls up some weeds. She turns over some earth. Then she makes a row of little holes in the dirt.

In Mary's basket are some seeds. One by one, Mary takes a seed from her basket. Plop! Into the earth it falls. Then Mary covers the seed with dirt. Plop! Plop! Plop!

Mary is happy as she works. She sings a song. She adds some of her love to each seed.

Now Mary has planted all the seeds. She turns to go back into the house. But standing before her is a young man. She has never seen him before.

"Oh!" says Mary, surprised.

"Please, Mary," says the young man. "God is with you, Mary. He has blessed you."

"What do you mean?" asks Mary. She does not yet understand that the young man is God's angel, Gabriel. She is frightened.

"Don't be afraid, Mary," says the young man in a quiet voice. "God has chosen you for something special. You will give birth to a son. You will name him Jesus. He will be the Son of God. He will be the king of his people forever. His Kingdom will never end."

"But how can this be?" Mary asks Gabriel.

"God's power will come upon you, Mary," Gabriel answers her. "Remember, there is nothing God cannot do."

Mary knows well that God can do anything. After all, God had saved her people more than once. God had loved her people. He had given them laws. Mary knows a lot about God. And now, Mary knows God is showing her a very special love. God is choosing her to be the mother of a special child. This child will someday be important to the Jewish people. What a lot God is asking of Mary!

Mary is a little scared. Then she remembers that God will always be with her. He will help her care for this special child.

"Oh, yes," says Mary. "I am God's helper. Of course, let it all be, just as you have said."

Gabriel smiles. Then as quickly as he had come, he goes away. Mary smiles to herself. She isn't frightened anymore.

Luke 1:26-38

2

SHEPHERDS VISIT A KING

The Bible tells us about Jesus' birth. But let's imagine that we are with Mary and Joseph when their baby son is born.

It is just getting dark. Joseph and Mary are entering the city gates of Bethlehem. Now that the sun has set, it is getting cool.

Joseph and Mary have traveled from Nazareth. They will list their names in Bethlehem. The Roman government wants to know the name of every person in the country.

"Joseph," says Mary. "I must tell you something."

"Mary, I know you are tired," says Joseph. He hugs Mary. "It has been a long trip, and it's getting cold."

"It's more than that, Joseph," says Mary. "I think the baby will be born tonight."

Joseph's face lights up in a big smile. "How wonderful!" he says. "The baby will be born at last."

But then Joseph frowns. "Oh, no!" he says. "Here we are, miles from home, and we don't even have a place to stay. Come, Mary. We must hurry to the nearest inn." Joseph is worried.

Mary and Joseph try the nearest inn. Then they try another and another. But every inn in the town of Bethlehem is full. There is no room for Mary and Joseph. There is no room for the baby who is about to be born.

"But, sir," says Joseph to the last innkeeper. "My wife is about to have a child. Surely you will not leave us in the street for the birth of the child!"

"Oh, dear, no!" says the innkeeper. "Come this way."

Mary and Joseph smile. At last they will have a room in the inn for the baby. They follow the innkeeper down the hall past many rooms.

"Will he stop at this room?" Mary wonders.

"Surely this next room will be ours," thinks Joseph.

But the innkeeper does not stop at any room. He goes right out the back door. "Here you are," he says, pointing to his stable. "There is plenty of clean straw. That is all I can do."

Joseph is upset. "Do you want us to stay in a stable?" he asks the innkeeper.

But Mary touches Joseph's arm. "Joseph," says Mary. "I'm sure there is enough straw for us to be comfortable. We will be warm. We will have a roof over our heads. It's all right."

Joseph looks at Mary's gentle face. Her sweet smile seems to fill the evening with sunshine. He knows why he loves her so much. "Very well," Joseph says to the innkeeper.

A few hours later, Mary holds the new baby boy in her arms. She is a little tired, but her smile lights up the stable.

"Look at him kick," says Joseph with pride. "He's going to be a strong man."

"But he holds my finger so softly. Jesus will be gentle too," says Mary.

"Strong and gentle," says Joseph. "That is a good way for a man to be." He tickles the baby's toes.

But what is happening? A man is coming to the stable. He is dressed in rough, old clothes. "Excuse me," he says to Mary and Joseph. "I have come to see the child. And some friends have come with me. May we all see the baby?"

"Of course," says Mary. "But I don't understand how you know about my baby."

"We will explain," says the man. He calls his

friends. They hurry to the stable. Some of the men carry baby lambs with them. "As you can see," says the man, "we are shepherds. Tonight we were taking care of our sheep just as we do every night. It is quiet work. Nothing much ever happens."

"Tonight something happened," says a second shepherd. "Suddenly the dark sky became very bright."

"It was an angel!" says a third shepherd.

"And the angel told us we would find a baby here," says a fourth shepherd.

"But not just any baby. The angel said it was a special baby!" says the first shepherd. "This baby brings joy to all of us tonight. He will grow up to be our king."

The shepherds are so happy. Thanks to the angel, they are the first to see the new king! One by one they come up to look at Jesus, the special baby. They each say a prayer of thanks. Some of the shepherds leave a lamb as a gift. Mary thanks them. Joseph makes sure no one comes too close to the baby.

Mary remembers the angel Gabriel. She remembers how Gabriel told her about Jesus. He said Jesus would be God's Son. He told her Jesus would be the king of his people forever. Now an angel has told these shepherds the same thing.

Mary knows God is watching over the stable. God is taking good care of her and Joseph and the baby. Mary smiles her sunshine smile.

Luke 2:8-20

3
THE STAR THAT LED TO A KING

Let's imagine what happens after the shepherds leave the stable. Mary and Joseph and the new baby are very tired. They need to rest. Mary and Joseph decide to stay in the stable for a few more days.

Many miles away, some special people are on their way for a visit. The little family has no idea that they are coming.

For many years, these special people have been looking for a sign in the sky. They are very wise men called magi (mā′jī). They are a little bit like scientists and a little bit like magicians.

Now, the magi know that a special sign up in the sky often means that something special is happening on earth. An old star may die. A new star may be born. Or a flash of light may speed across the sky. Then the magi know that maybe an old king has died. Or maybe a special child has been born. Such a child may grow up to be the leader of many people.

One night, far, far up in the sky, the wise magi see two large stars come together. The two large stars look like one giant star. They light up the whole sky. It is as bright as day.

The magi are excited. "What can this mean?" asks one.

"It must be something important!" says another.

"I believe it is the birth of a king," says a third.

The oldest and wisest magi says, "I believe a special child has been born under this star. This child will be the king of many people."

"One thing is for sure," says one of the magi. "We must go see. We must follow the star."

"Of course," say the others. "Let us set off on our journey tonight."

So the wise magi pack up their camels. They pack food and clean clothes for the trip. They also pack many gifts in case they do find a new king. They pack gold and silver and jewels. They pack the finest oils and spices. They pack sweet-smelling scents.

The magi set out to follow the star. They travel for many days and many nights. Each day they get a little closer to the star. The journey is long. The magi are tired from the long trip. But they do not give up. They hope their journey will be rewarded. They hope they will see the child who will someday lead so many people.

Finally, the magi arrive at the small town of Bethlehem. The star is almost above them.

"Can a king be born in this poor town?" asks one of the magi.

"There is no palace. There is no fine building at all," says another.

The magi make their way through the streets. They walk toward the brightest part of town. It is as bright as day from the star.

The magi go down one street. Then they go down another and then . . . Before them is a stable. Cows and donkeys are eating hay. Small lambs are napping. In the center of the stable, a man is sitting near a woman. The woman is holding a small baby.

The magi look at the child. They look at one another. This is the end of their journey. They have found the king. They fall on their knees and thank God. The magi worship the child. They offer their wonderful gifts.

Mary and Joseph are surprised and happy that visitors have come so far to see the baby Jesus. They are beginning to understand that Jesus will be the king of many people.

Over the stable, the star still lights up the sky.

Matthew 2:1-11

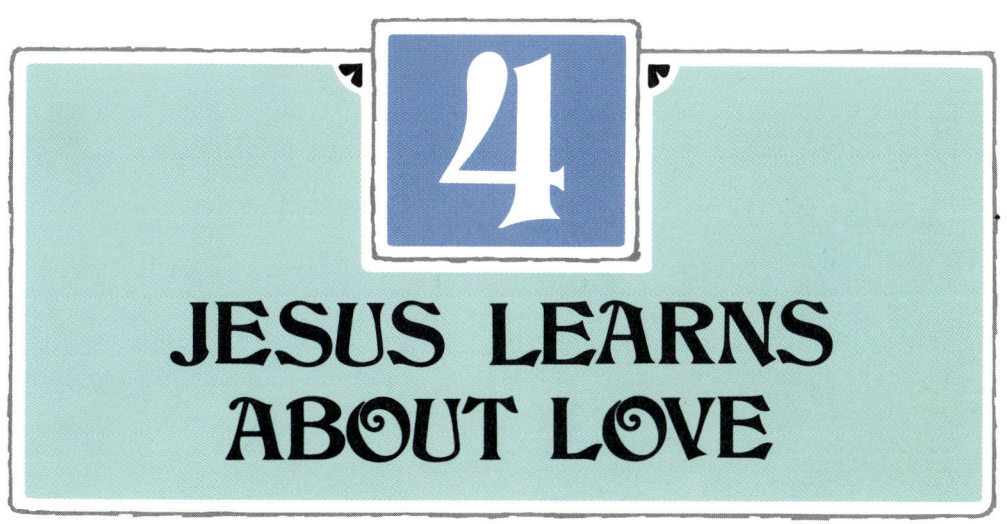

JESUS LEARNS ABOUT LOVE

It is hard to think about Jesus when he was a little boy. But he was your age once long ago. Life was very different when Jesus was a child. Still, he did many of the things you do today. He helped his mother. He helped his father.

Let's imagine a day in Jesus' life. It is late in the morning. Joseph has been at work for several hours. His woodshop is right next to the house. He likes to start work early in the morning. It is still cool then. Now, it is very warm.

Look who is helping Joseph. It is Jesus. They are making a chair. Jesus holds a nail. Joseph gives it a sharp tap with his hammer. Now the nail is set. Jesus can move his hand away. Tap! Tap! Tap! Joseph hammers the nail into the wood. Jesus gets another nail ready.

Jesus likes to help Joseph. He wants to be a carpenter when he grows up. He wants to be just like Joseph.

Soon the chair is finished. Joseph begins to saw wood for a new table. Jesus gets a broom. He sweeps up the sawdust after Joseph has sawed the wood. Then Joseph picks up a plane. He slides the plane over the wood. Long curls of wood fall to the floor. Jesus sweeps them up.

"Jesus," says Joseph. "I'm getting hungry. How about you?"

"I sure am," Jesus answers. It seems that he is just about always hungry these days.

"Tell your mother I'll be right there," says Joseph.

Jesus goes next door. His mother, Mary, turns when she hears him come in. "Someone must be ready for lunch," she says. She gives him a hug and a kiss.

Jesus smiles and nods.

"The soup is just ready," says Mary. "Would you put some bowls and spoons on the table, please?"

Jesus does as Mary asks. A pitcher of milk is on the table. A loaf of warm, fresh-baked bread stands beside a pot of sweet butter.

While Mary slices the bread, Jesus walks over to the oven. The fire in the oven has died down. Jesus decides to help his mother. He will build the fire back up. Jesus picks up some thin pieces of wood from beside the oven. He puts them on the hot ashes inside the oven.

"Ouch!" cries Jesus. The wood catches fire so fast it burns his hand.

Mary hurries over and grabs Jesus' hand. She puts it into a bucket of water standing nearby. "What happened?" she asks as she holds his hand in the water.

Jesus does not want to answer his mother. He knows he should not be doing anything with fire. But he wants to tell Mary the truth.

"I put some wood in the oven. The fire had burned down," says Jesus, looking at the floor.

Mary takes Jesus' hand out of the water and dries it. She kisses it gently. Then she holds it in her own soft, strong hand.

"Your hand will be all right, Jesus," says Mary.

"But you shouldn't go so close to the oven. I know you wanted to help. But it's not safe. You are too young. You can help me in other ways." Mary kisses Jesus' hand again. She hugs him close to her.

Jesus feels better. His mother's healing love makes the hurt go away.

5
JESUS IN HIS FATHER'S HOUSE

It is the feast of Passover in Jerusalem. Passover is an important Jewish feast. People from all over have come to the city to celebrate.

Passover is a special time for Jewish children. During Passover they learn the story of how God helped their people. Oh, look! There are Mary and Joseph and Jesus. They are in that crowd of people. They must have just finished their Passover meal. Everyone is headed toward the city gate.

Oh! Now they have disappeared in the crowd. Let's hurry and catch up with them. Then we can see what happens on their way home to Nazareth.

Mary and Joseph are walking just up ahead. They are talking and laughing with their friends. What a good Passover feast this has been.

Mary leaves Joseph's side and begins to walk back. She seems to be looking for someone. She stops to ask some friends a question. "Have you seen Jesus?" she asks.

The friends shake their heads. "No, I have not seen him since we left Jerusalem," says one.

Mary smiles and thanks them. She continues to walk back toward the city. Along the way she stops to ask people if they have seen her son.

When Mary has talked to all the people she is traveling with, she stops. A frown wrinkles her forehead and pulls down the corners of her mouth. She turns and hurries back to Joseph.

"Joseph, Joseph," Mary cries, grabbing his sleeve. "I can't find Jesus."

Joseph looks at Mary. She is not easily upset. But she is very upset now. Joseph looks ahead. He can see that Jesus is not with the people in front of them. He looks back toward all the people Mary has just talked to.

"Jesus must be back there with some of our friends," Joseph says.

"No," says Mary. "He is not. I've asked everyone. No one has even seen Jesus since we left the city."

"Then he must be back in Jerusalem!" Joseph grabs Mary's hand. Together they run back to Jerusalem. They pass friends and other travelers who are leaving the city.

Joseph and Mary hurry through the city. They look for Jesus down narrow streets and in small shops. They ask almost everyone they see if he or she has seen Jesus.

"He's about this tall," says Joseph, holding a hand to his chest.

"He's twelve," says Mary. "He has brown hair and brown eyes."

"He's wearing a yellow shirt," says Joseph.

"He has a nice smile," says Mary.

Much, much later, Mary and Joseph have still not found Jesus. They are tired. They are hot. They are thirsty. They know it will soon be dark. They cannot look for Jesus after night falls.

Joseph and Mary walk slowly down a street, hand in hand. Mary's eyes fill with tears. Then she notices the building in front of them.

"Oh, Joseph, look," she says. "The Temple. Let's go in and pray."

Joseph nods. "Prayer will help," he says. Mary and Joseph are tired. But they hurry into the Temple.

Inside it is cooler. The light is dim. In a corner, a group of men are talking. Mary and Joseph walk toward the group. They want to ask the men if they have seen Jesus.

As Mary and Joseph come closer, they see that Jesus is right in the middle of the men. He is talking to them. He is listening to them and asking questions. And the men are listening to Jesus and asking him questions, too. They are amazed at how much this young boy knows about God and about his religion.

"Jesus," says Mary. She rushes forward. "My son, why have you done this? We have been so worried. We have been looking all over for you."

Jesus looks up at Mary and Joseph. "Why did you have to look for me?" he asks. "Didn't you know I had to be in my Father's house?"

Joseph and Mary do not know what to think of Jesus' answer. They only know they are glad to have found their son.

Luke 2:41-51

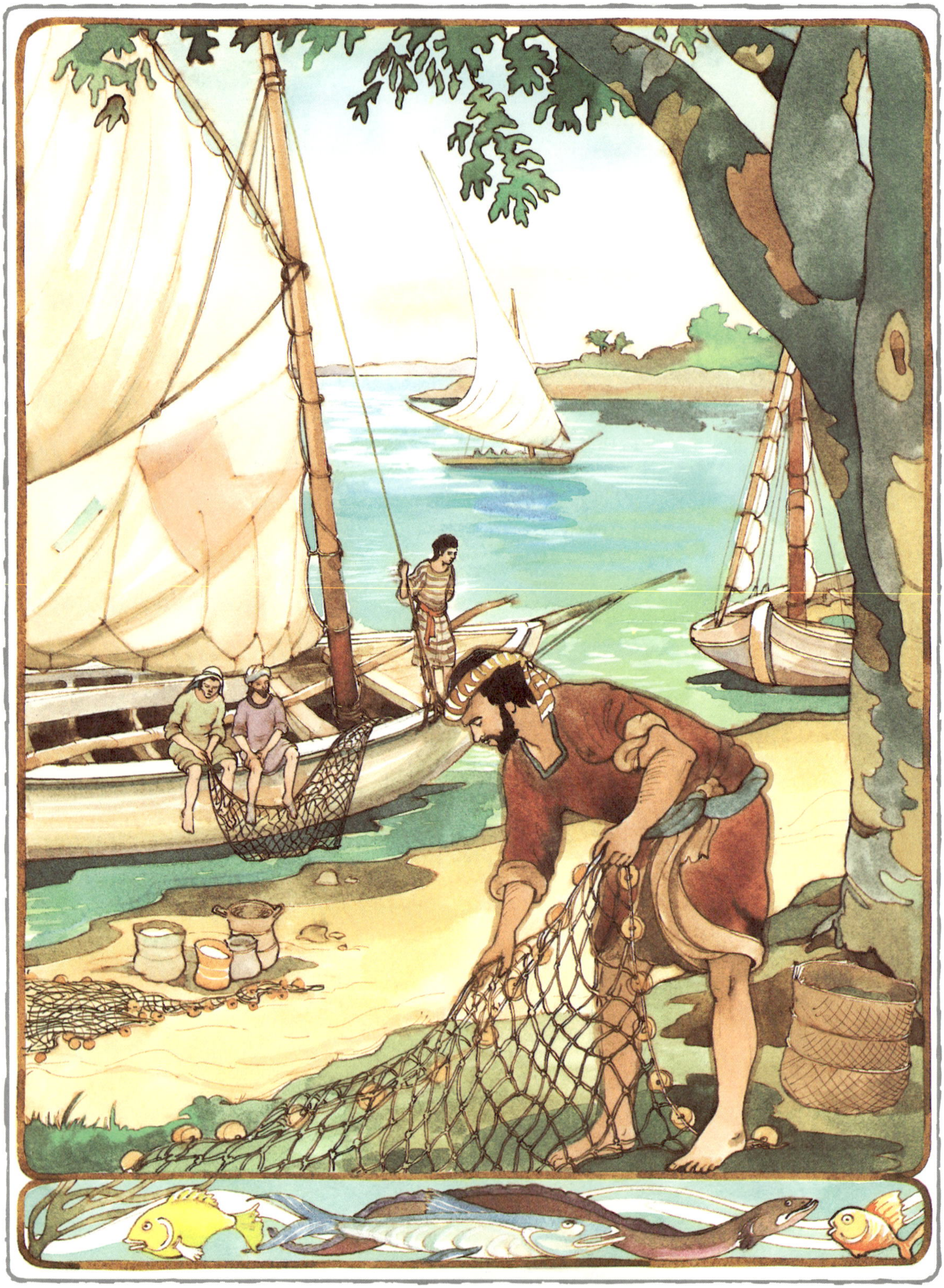

6
THOSE WHO FOLLOW JESUS

We know that Jesus is our good friend. But Jesus also had many friends when he lived on earth. Let's think about some of the special people who were Jesus' friends then.

Think back long ago. Imagine you are on the shores of a large lake. It is still early in the morning. There are boats all around. They are pulled up on the sand. Fishermen are washing their nets. The fishermen are unhappy. They did not catch a single fish all night. They look sad.

Now a stranger is walking along the beach. He is coming toward the fishermen. Some men and women are following the stranger. Children are running along beside him. It is Jesus. But the fishermen don't know this.

Jesus walks up to a fisherman named Simon Peter. "May I use your boat for a little while?" he asks.

"Why not!" says Simon. "It isn't doing me any good. I haven't caught a fish in days."

Jesus gets into the boat. "Please push me out a ways," he says. Simon does so. Jesus begins to talk to the crowd of people. They sit on the shore and listen.

At first Simon Peter and the other fishermen turn their backs on Jesus. They keep working on their nets. But soon they hear Jesus talk about God's love. They drop their nets and walk down to the shore to join the crowd. They listen carefully. The stranger seems so kind and wise.

Soon Jesus rows to shore. He speaks to Simon and his brother, Andrew. "Go back out in your boats," he says. "You will catch fish."

"Impossible!" says Simon. But Jesus is looking at him with peace and love. Suddenly Simon thinks Jesus may be right.

"Well, if you say so," Simon says. He calls to the other fishermen. Soon they all set out into the water.

"Go out where it is deep," says Jesus. "Then let down your nets."

Simon and Andrew and their friends James and John do as Jesus says. So do the other fishermen. Look! What is happening? Everyone is shouting. They sound happy. The fishermen are pulling in their nets. And the nets are filled with fish!

"The boats might go down with this load of fish," laughs John. All the fishermen who were so sad before are now happy. Jesus stands on the beach and smiles.

Soon the fishermen row to shore. Simon Peter pulls his boat up on the sand. Then he falls to his knees before Jesus. "Please, Lord," he says. "I do not always do what God wants me to do."

Jesus lays a hand on Simon's head. "Do not be afraid," he says. "Stand up now. I want you to join me in a new job." Jesus turns to all the fishermen. "Soon you can all be fishing for men and women."

Jesus turns and walks away. In less than a minute, Simon, Andrew, James, John, and all the rest of the fishermen follow him. They do not look back at their boats or nets.

The fishermen follow Jesus into town. They talk about what they heard Jesus say earlier.

"Loving others really is the best thing we can do," says Andrew.

"Yes. We all must love everyone," another fisherman says.

Just then, Jesus stops in front of an office. The man inside is named Levi. No one likes Levi. He makes people give him money. The money he takes is tax money for the government. Jesus enters Levi's office and begins to talk with him.

"What is this?" asks James. "Why is Jesus talking to Levi? He knows that Levi takes money from all of us!"

"I think Jesus is just going to use old Levi as a bad example for us. He will use Levi as an example of how not to be," says John.

"I think you are both wrong," says another fisherman.

"So do I," says Simon. "Don't you remember what Jesus said this morning? It's not a great thing to love people who are easy to love."

"That's right," Andrew says. "We should love people who are hard to love!"

James and John know that they have been wrong. Soon Levi follows Jesus out of his office. He joins the group of fishermen. James and John go out of their way to be nice to him.

But what is happening now? Jesus is talking to a group of women.

"This is too much," says Andrew.

One of the other fishermen speaks out. "You are forgetting something else Jesus told us today," he says. "Remember when he said that God loves *everyone?*"

"That's right," says James. "We are all God's children. Jesus loves these women just as he loves us. I want these women to join us."

Soon Jesus walks on. The women are happy to walk along with Jesus and the other men. Andrew is very nice to them.

Luke 5:1-11, 27-28; 8:1-3

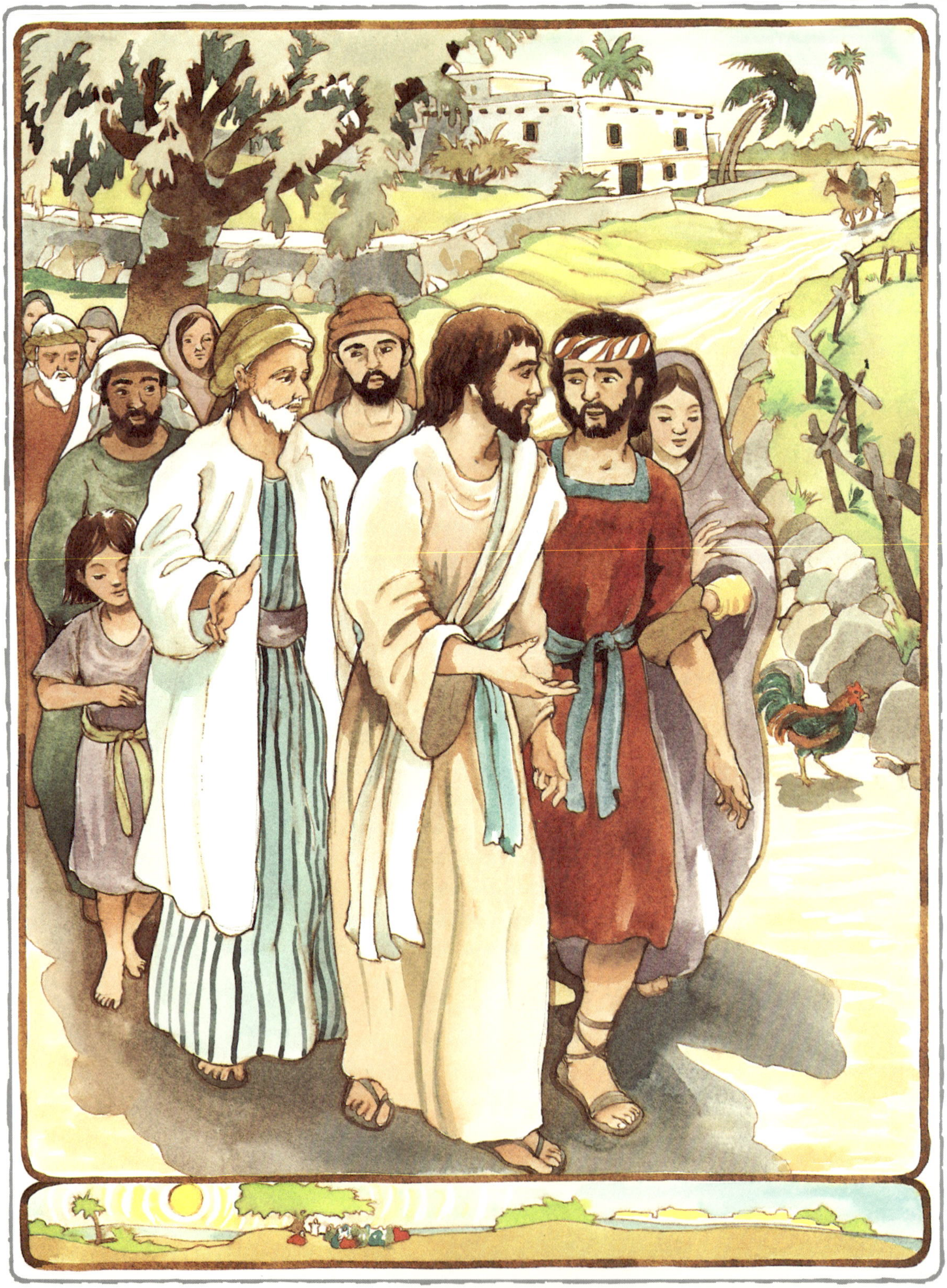

7
JESUS TEACHES ABOUT GOD'S LOVE

When Jesus was living on earth, he did not spend much time alone. Most of the time he was with his friends. But he was often with other people, too.

People from all over had heard about Jesus. They wanted to come and listen to him. They wanted to learn from Jesus because he was such a good teacher.

Let's imagine a day long, long ago. Jesus is walking with his friends. The sun beats down on them. Every step they take stirs up dust around them.

As they go along, many people recognize Jesus. They stop what they are doing and follow him. They hope they will learn from Jesus. Some of the people run off to tell others that he is coming. Soon a crowd gathers around Jesus.

The crowd is so noisy. Many people cannot hear what Jesus is saying. Jesus sees some trees up the road. He decides to stop there. Then everyone can sit in the shade and hear him.

The people find places to sit on the grass under the trees. They become very quiet. They don't want to miss a single word Jesus has to say.

Soon Jesus begins to speak. He tells everyone he is going to teach about God's love. Jesus has a special way of teaching. He teaches by telling stories. Let's listen to the first story Jesus tells today.

"This is a story that could happen to any of you," Jesus says. "What if you had one hundred sheep? And what if you lost one? What would you do? How would you feel?"

A man on the edge of the crowd answers Jesus.

The man is wearing nice clothes. "What can it matter to lose one sheep?" he asks.

Many people in the crowd are not so rich. They say, "Oh, but we are poor. We cannot afford to lose even one sheep."

Jesus smiles. Then he goes on with his story. "When a shepherd loses even one sheep out of one hundred, he is sad. He leaves all the others and goes looking for the one sheep. He knows that the one sheep is special. It is as important as the rest. He looks and looks until he finds the one sheep. Then he is so happy that he brings the sheep home. He asks all his friends and neighbors to come and celebrate."

The crowd is very, very still. They like Jesus' story. Jesus continues. "It is the same way with God, your Father," he says. "When even one of you turns away from him, he will look and look for you. He knows each of you is special and important. When he finds you, he takes you home with him. Then there is great joy in heaven."

The story is over. Now the people talk quietly to each other. "What a good storyteller Jesus is," they say. "It is true," they say. "God does love us just like that. God loves us very much."

When the crowd is quiet once more, Jesus begins a new story.

"Imagine a woman who has ten silver coins," says Jesus. "The coins mean a lot to her. But one day, when she counts them, she finds that one is gone. What does she do?"

Again the rich man speaks up. "What is one coin among many?" he asks.

But others in the crowd do not agree. "Every coin matters to us," they say. "We need them all."

Jesus goes on with his story. "Well," he says. "The woman knows the one coin is important. She looks and looks for her coin. She looks until she finds it. And when she does find it, she is so happy. She goes to her friends and says, 'Let's celebrate!' So I tell you this. God celebrates when just one person comes back to him."

Again the people talk about how good God's love is. Then Jesus begins another story.

"Once a man had two sons," Jesus says. "The younger son was unhappy. He wanted to try living away from home. So he asked his father for some money. The father was sad to see his son leave. But he gladly gave him the money.

"At first the young man had a good time. He had many friends. He spent his money on fun things to do. But one day his money ran out. Then his friends went away. He had to earn money by feeding pigs.

"As the young man worked one day, he thought about his home. He thought about his father. He wanted to go back home.

"Now, the young man's father watched for his son every day. One day he finally saw his son walking toward home. He ran out to meet him. He was so happy to see his son. He had a big party to celebrate."

The people like Jesus' story. They know that the father in the story is just like God. They understand that God waits for those people who turn away from him. They know that God celebrates when people return to him. They know that God thinks each person is special.

The air is getting cooler. Soon it will be evening. People begin to make their way home. They talk to each other about how much they have learned about God's love. They talk about what a good teacher Jesus is.

Luke 15:4-24

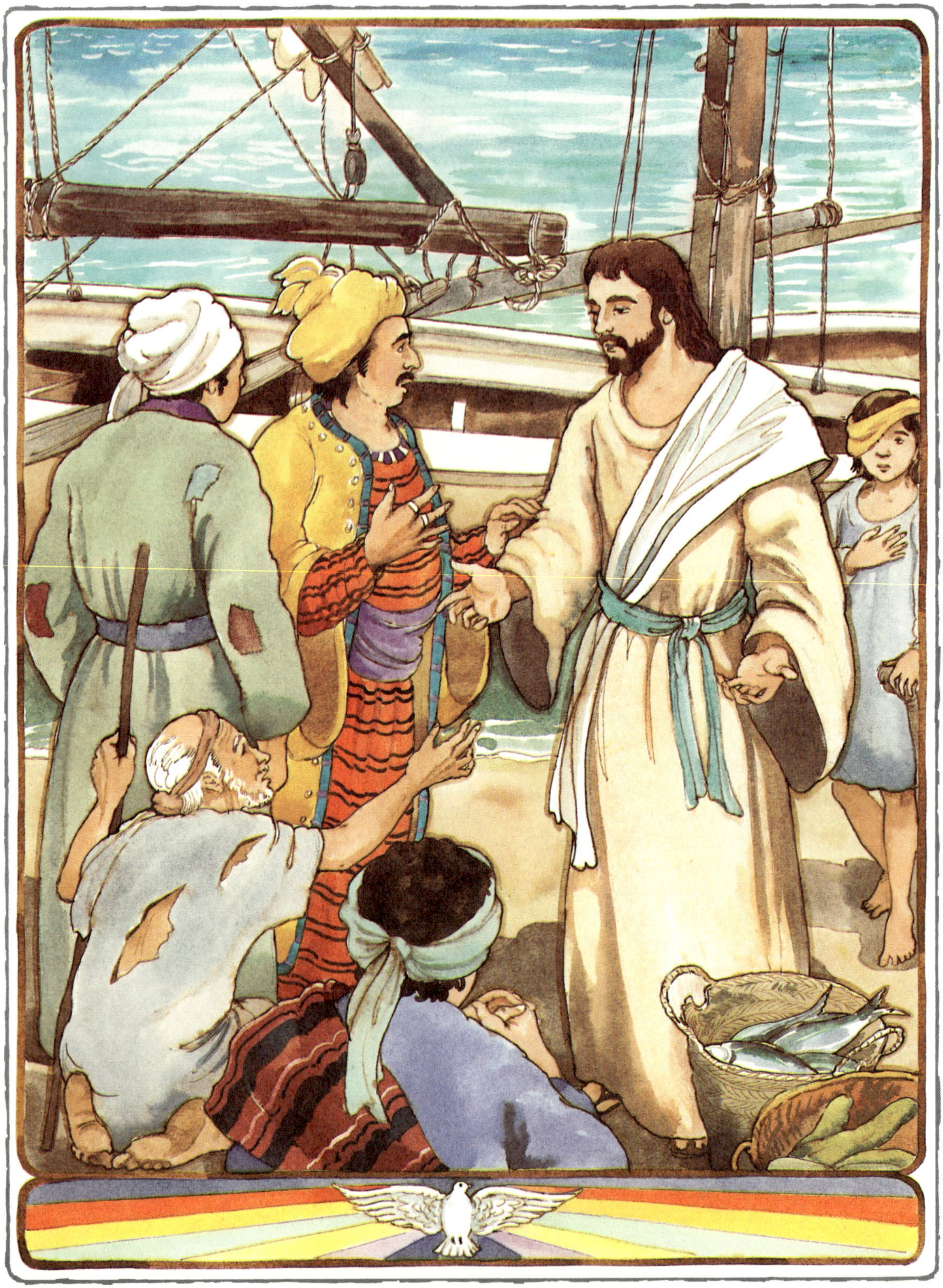

8

JESUS' HEALING LOVE

Jesus is known as more than just a teacher. He is also known as a healer. A healer is someone who makes people well. Often the crowds who followed Jesus were filled with sick people. Some of them could not walk or see or hear.

The people knew that Jesus could heal them. He could make blind people see. He could make lame people walk. He could make people who were sad or hurt feel good again. Jesus could heal people with his loving words and touch.

Let's imagine a day long ago. Jesus is on the shores of Lake Galilee. Many people have come to hear him teach. Some have come to be healed. Many of the people are poor. Their clothes are old and worn. But they want to learn from Jesus. They believe he can heal them.

What is this? A man is pushing his way through the crowd. He seems upset. He is not dressed like a poor man. Oh, it is Jairus. Jairus is an important man. He is speaking to Jesus. He is almost crying.

"Jesus," says Jairus. "Please, please come with me. My daughter is sick. She is so sick. I am afraid she might die. Jesus, I've heard that if you just touch people they are well again. Please come and lay your hands on my little girl so that she may get well."

Jesus puts a hand on Jairus' arm and nods. Jairus turns and starts toward home. He is happy that Jesus is going with him. Now there is a good chance that his little child will be saved. "Jesus is a good man," Jairus thinks to himself.

Jesus follows closely behind Jairus. Then suddenly he stops and turns around. "Who has just touched my robe?" he asks.

A woman in the crowd comes slowly forward. She falls on her knees in front of Jesus. "I touched your robe, Lord," she says.

The woman has tears in her eyes. They are tears of happiness. "I have been ill for twelve years," she says. "I came today so that you could touch me and heal me. But you were leaving so quickly there was no chance. I thought that if I could touch your robe, I would be healed. So I did. And look! I am well!"

Jesus smiles down at the woman. He tells her, "Your faith has made you well. Go now in peace."

Jairus has watched all this. Now he is sure Jesus can help. "This woman touched Jesus' robe and was healed," Jairus thinks. "I am sure that when Jesus touches my daughter, she will live!"

But look! One of Jairus' servants is running down the street. Here he comes through the crowd of people. He stops before Jairus. Tears come to his eyes as he speaks.

"Master," says the servant. "It is too late. Your daughter has died. Send Jesus back. It is too late."

Jairus looks as if his world has ended. But Jesus speaks to him. "Don't listen to that," he says. "And don't be afraid, Jairus. Only believe."

"But Lord—" Jairus starts to say.

Jesus puts a finger to his lips to quiet Jairus. Jesus turns to his friends Peter, James, and John. "Only you three come with Jairus and me," he says. Then he takes Jairus' hand and hurries off.

When they get to Jairus' house, everyone is crying and running about. The family is upset. The servants are sad. Jesus speaks to the people. "What is going on?" he asks. "Why are you all crying and running about? The little girl is not dead. She is only asleep."

The servants and the family do not even listen to Jesus. Some of them make fun of him. Jesus takes Jairus and his wife and his own three friends into the little girl's room.

Jesus walks over to the bed. The little girl lies very still. Her eyes are closed. Jairus holds his wife in his arms. She is crying.

Jesus takes the little girl by the hand. "Little One," he says. "I want you to get up now."

The little child sits up and looks around. She wonders who the kind man is. She wonders why her mother and father have tears in their eyes.

Jesus walks toward the door. He stops to say something to Jairus and his wife. "Don't forget to give her something to eat!" he says.

Mark 5:21-43

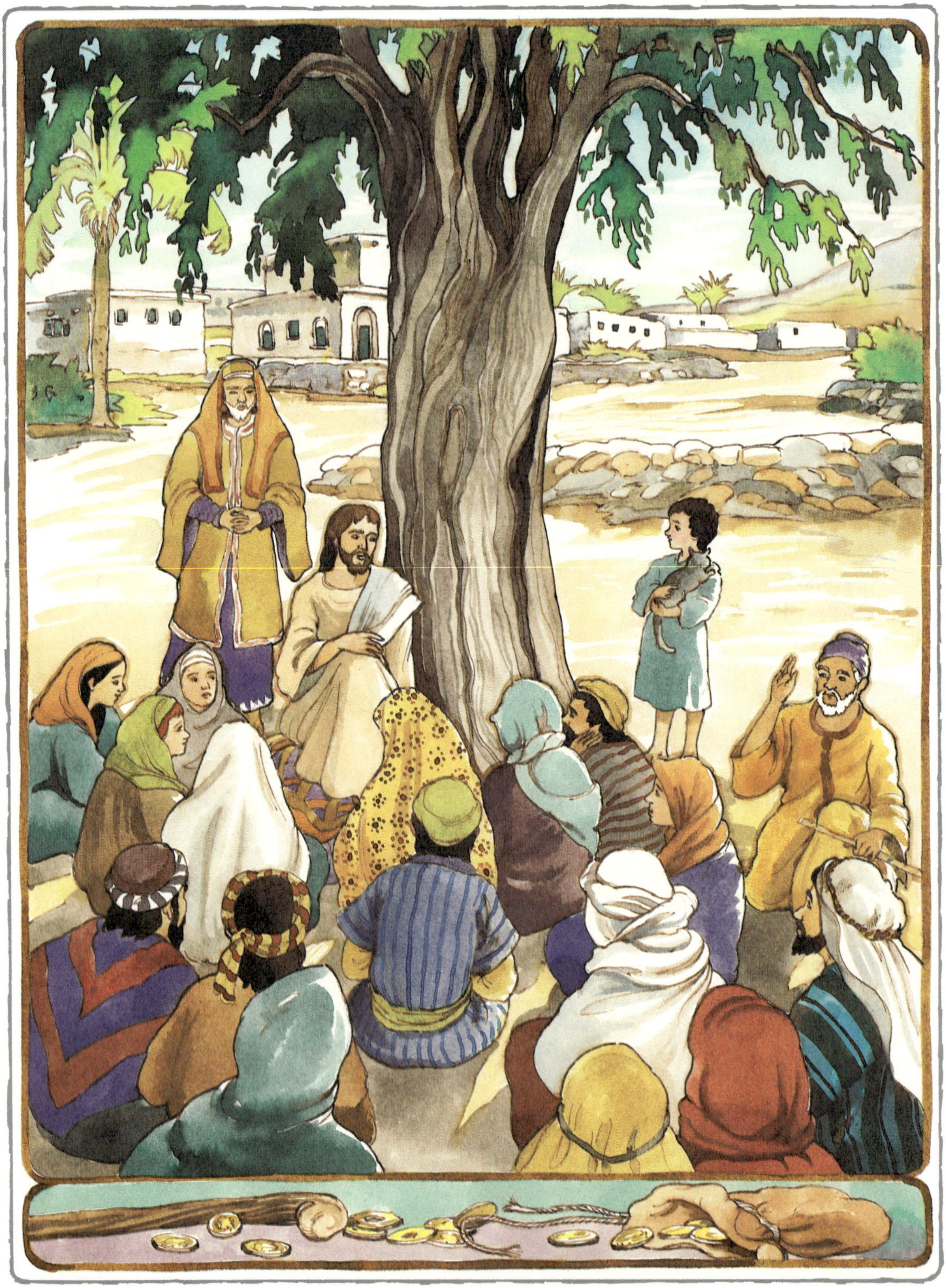

9

JESUS' STORY ABOUT A GOOD NEIGHBOR

Sometimes Jesus taught the people who followed him. Sometimes he healed people who were sick or hurt. Sometimes Jesus told stories about his Father's love.

Most people who listened to Jesus liked him. They wanted to hear his words. But some people tried to trick Jesus. Imagine that you are with Jesus one day when someone tries to trick him.

There is Jesus now. He is sitting with many people. They are listening to him. Jesus is talking about how much his Father loves them. He tells the people that God gives them love and life forever.

But look! A man is pushing through the crowd of people. He comes right up to Jesus.

"Teacher," he says. "Tell me how to have life forever."

Jesus knows the man wants to trick him. So he asks the man a question. "How does the Bible answer your question?" he asks.

"Well," says the man. "The Bible says I must love God with all my heart and soul. I must love God with all my strength and mind. I must also love my neighbor, just as I love myself."

"You are right," says Jesus. "Do that and you will live always."

But the man is not happy with the answer. He still wants to trick Jesus. "Well then," he says. "Who is my neighbor?"

Jesus is not worried by the man's question. He has a story to tell everyone. The story is about being a good neighbor.

"Once a man was traveling between towns," says Jesus.

The people around Jesus smile. They are happy that he is going to tell them a story.

"But robbers came after the man," says Jesus. "They beat him. They took his money. They left him hurt by the side of the road."

The people in the crowd shake their heads. They think that the robbers were bad to act the way they did.

Jesus goes on. "Soon a priest came by. He saw the hurt man by the road, but he crossed to the other side. He went on his way. He did not stop to help."

"How terrible!" says someone in the crowd.

Jesus goes on with his story. "Soon another man came along," says Jesus. "He stopped to look at the hurt man. But he went right on, too. Finally a Samaritan came along. [Samaritans were people from a place called Samaria.] The Samaritan saw the hurt man. He felt sorry for him. He went over to help him."

The people in the crowd smile. They are happy to know that some people want to help others.

"The Samaritan cleaned the hurt man's sores with wine and oil," says Jesus. "The Samaritan wrapped the sores with bandages. Then he lifted the hurt man onto his donkey. He took the man to the next town. Now, the Samaritan had to travel on. But he took the hurt man to an inn. He gave money to the innkeeper. He told the innkeeper to take good care of the hurt man. He said he would be back to pay more later."

"What a wonderful man," says someone in the crowd. "What a good thing to do," says another person. "We should all act that way," says someone else.

Jesus smiles. He knows that the people in the crowd understand. He likes to tell them stories about God. He likes to tell people how his Father wants them to act.

Jesus turns to the man who is trying to trick him. He asks the man a question. "Which one of the men acted like a neighbor?"

The man answers, "The neighbor was the Samaritan. The man who was kind and helpful was the neighbor."

Jesus looks at the man. "Then you go," Jesus says. "And act like a good neighbor."

Luke 10:25-37

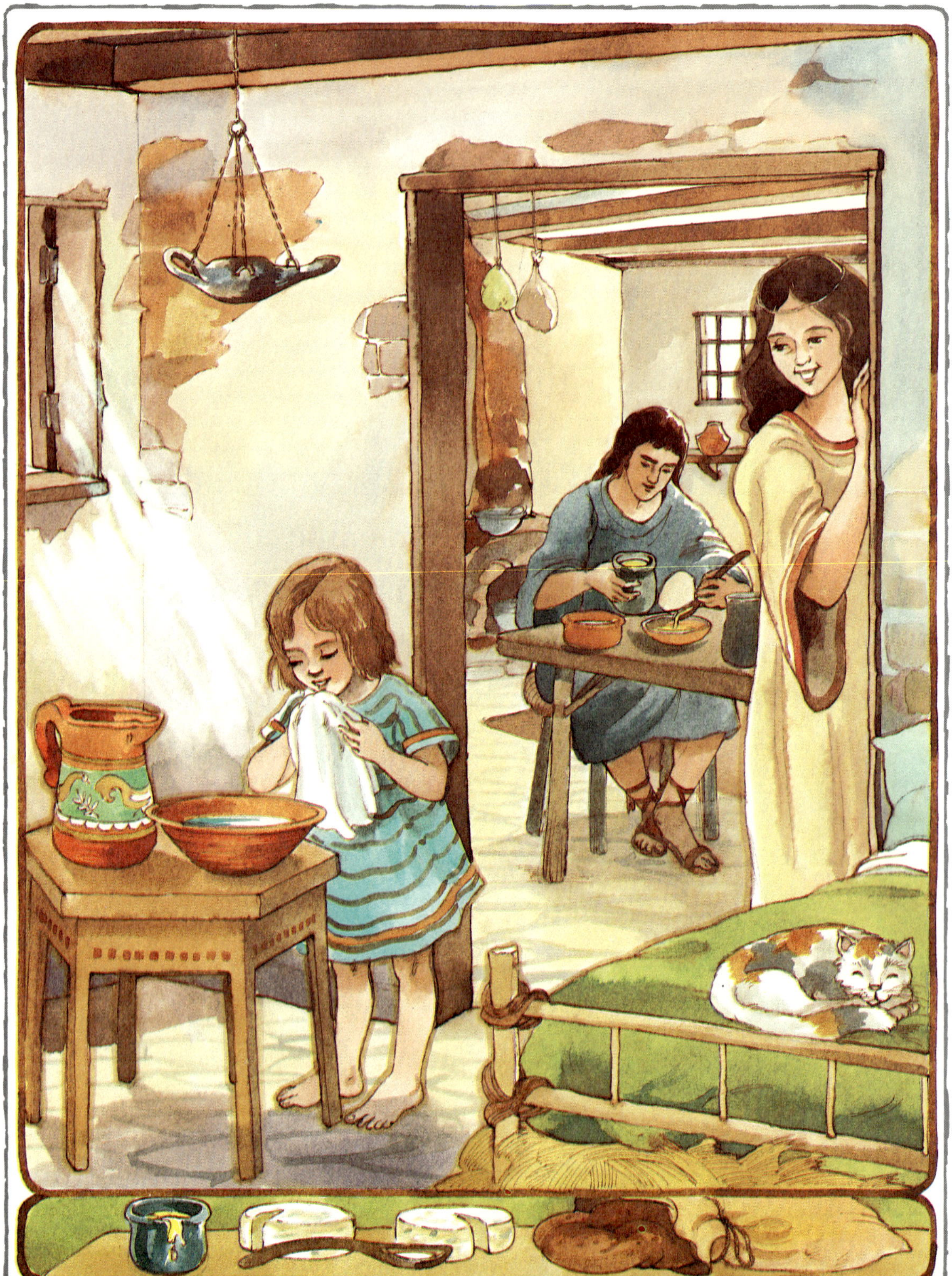

10
JESUS LOVES THE LITTLE CHILDREN

Jesus was once a little child himself. And when he grew to be a man, he loved little children.

Imagine that you are a child many, many years ago. It is the time when Jesus lived on earth. Imagine that you wake up one morning. You know right away that it is a special day.

"Hurry, hurry," says your mother. "Get up right now and come to breakfast."

You quickly put your clothes on. There is a bowl of water beside the door. You splash some water on your face.

Your father is already at the table. He puts a piece of bread in a bowl for you. He pours warm milk over it. He dips a spoon into a stone jar. Then he tips the spoon over your bread and milk. Golden honey pours from the spoon, catching the early morning sunlight. Yes, it is a special day when you get honey for breakfast.

Your mother is putting some bread and cheese into a goatskin bag. That means someone is going away for the day. The food is for the noon meal.

"Are you going somewhere?" you ask your father.

"Yes," he answers with a smile. "But I'm not going alone."

You see that your mother is putting a lot of bread and cheese into the goatskin bag. "Are you going with Daddy?" you ask your mother.

"Yes," says your mother with a smile. "But I'm not going alone."

Now you know why it is a special day. Your parents are going away. And they are taking you with them.

"Where are we going? When can we leave? What are we going to do? Why are we going?" You are filled with questions. You are so excited. You bounce up and down on your chair.

"A man called Jesus is visiting the next town. We are going to see and hear him," says your father.

"He is a wise teacher," says your mother.

"He heals people who are sick," says your father.

"He tells people about God's love," says your mother. "And he should know about God. People say he is God's Son."

Now you are really excited. "What are we waiting for?" you ask. "Let's go now. Can I carry our lunch?"

So you set off with your parents. You walk to the next town. It is still early morning, but it is getting warm. It is very dusty. You notice that there are many people walking along toward the next town.

"Are all these people going to see Jesus, too?" you ask your parents.

They smile and nod at you. "What a special man Jesus must be," you think.

As you come into the town, more and more people fill the road. Everyone is walking toward the center of town. There is plenty of shade there from the many olive trees.

People are sitting on the grass under the trees. They are eating their lunches.

Your family finds a place to sit. You share the bread and cheese.

But now what? Everyone was talking a moment ago. Now everyone is quiet. You turn to see what is happening. A man is walking through the crowd of people. Some men and women are walking beside him.

"There he is," says your mother. "There is Jesus."

Some people reach out to touch Jesus as he goes by. He smiles. He touches the people who reach out. He looks at different people.

Suddenly Jesus looks at you. No one has ever looked at you that way before. All at once you jump up. You run toward Jesus. Many other children are also running toward him.

But what is this? Some of the men with Jesus grab you. "No, no," they say. "Go back to your parents. Don't bother Jesus."

You feel sad. You start walking back to your place. Then you hear Jesus' voice.

"No, James and John. Let the children be. Let them come to me. They want to see me, and I want to see them."

You turn back toward Jesus. He holds his arms out to you. Other children are starting to crowd around Jesus. They touch him and hug him. You climb right up into Jesus' lap.

It feels so good to have Jesus' arms around you. You can feel his love for you and for everyone. You look at the crowd. You can see your parents. Their mouths are open in surprise.

Now Jesus is speaking to all the people. "I wanted these little ones to come to me," he says. "My Father's Kingdom belongs to them. All of you grownups have much to learn from these children. Learn from them how to enter my Father's Kingdom. Then it can belong to you, too."

You sit on Jesus' lap. You feel proud of yourself to be a child. You feel so good that you want to sit on Jesus' lap forever.

Luke 18:15-17